WITHDRAWN

MONUMENTAL MILESTONES
GREAT EVENTS OF MODERN TIMES

Top Secret:
The Story of the
Manhattan Project

Mitchell Lane
PUBLISHERS

P.O. Box 196
Hockessin, Delaware 19707
www.mitchelllane.com

Titles in the Series

MONUMENTAL MILESTONES
GREAT EVENTS OF MODERN TIMES

Top Secret:
The Story of the
Manhattan Project

Kathleen Tracy

Copyright © 2006 by Mitchell Lane Publishers, Inc. All rights reserved. No part of this book may be reproduced without written permission from the publisher. Printed and bound in the United States of America.

Printing   1   2   3   4   5   6   7   8

Library of Congress Cataloging-in-Publication Data

Tracy, Kathleen.

Top secret: the story of the Manhattan Project / by Kathleen Tracy.

    p. cm. — (Monumental milestones: great events of modern times)

Includes bibliographical references and index.

ISBN 1-58415-399-7 (lib. bd.)

1. Manhattan Project (U.S.)—Juvenile literature. 2. Atomic bomb

United States—History—Juvenile literature. I. Title. II. Monumental milestones.

QC773.3.U5T73 2005

355.8'25119'0973—dc22   2004030310

ABOUT THE AUTHOR: Kathleen Tracy has been a journalist for over twenty years. Her writing has been featured in magazines including *The Toronto Star's* "Star Week," *A&E Biography* magazine, *KidScreen,* and *TVTimes.* She is also the author of numerous biographies including "The Boy Who Would be King" (Dutton), "Jerry Seinfeld - The Entire Domain" (Carol Publishing), "Don Imus - America's Cowboy" (Carroll & Graf), "Mariano Guadalupe Vallejo," and "William Hewlett: Pioneer of the Computer Age," both for Mitchell Lane. She has recently completed "Diana Rigg: The Biography" for Benbella Books.

PHOTO CREDITS: Cover, pp. 1, 3 Getty Images; p. 6 Library of Congress; p. 13 Science Researchers, p. 15 Corbis; p. 20 Getty Images; p. 25 National Archives at College Park, Maryland; p. 28 Library of Congress; p. 36 Getty Images

PUBLISHER'S NOTE: This story is based on the author's extensive research, which she believes to be accurate. Documentation of such research is contained on page 46.

The internet sites referenced herein were active as of the publication date. Due to the fleeting nature of some web sites, we cannot guarantee they will all be active when you are reading this book.

Contents

Top Secret:
The Story of the Manhattan Project

Kathleen Tracy

On December 7, 1941, a surprise attack by Japanese aircraft devastated America's Pacific Fleet moored at Pearl Harbor.

Of the 2,403 Americans who perished at Pearl Harbor, almost half died when the USS Arizona exploded and sank. Outraged by the attack, America immediately declared war on Japan, signaling the start of World War II.

A Day of Infamy

December 7, 1941 started out as a quiet Sunday morning on the Hawaiian island of Oahu. Docked at Pearl Harbor were 130 battleships, cruisers and destroyers, about half of the United States Navy's Pacific Fleet. Seven of the nine battleships were moored along what was called *Battleship Row* on the shore of Ford Island. Nearby was a Naval air station where hundreds of U.S. warplanes were parked.

Shortly before 7:00 A.M., the crew of the destroyer U.S.S. *Ward* had spotted a mini Japanese submarine trying to make its way into the harbor. They dropped depth charges which sunk the sub. They reported the incident to headquarters. A few minutes later, a radar station picked up signals indicating a large number of airplanes. But the controllers assumed it was the aircraft from an American carrier.

The first hint that the controllers had been terribly wrong was a noise. It began as a hum and then turned into a roar as Japanese planes suddenly appeared in the sky. At 7:53 A.M. the first bombs began to drop on Pearl Harbor. Although caught completely by surprise, the soldiers tried to fight back, manning their guns and trying to protect themselves and the fleet.

But because they were tied down, the battleships were particularly vulnerable. About twenty minutes into the attack, a bomb weighing nearly a ton struck the U.S.S. *Arizona* and caused a massive explosion.

Marine Corporal E.C. Nightingale was one of the few survivors of the *Arizona*. According to his eyewitness account, "I was the last man to leave secondary aft…The railings, as we ascended, were very hot and as we reached the boat deck I noted that it was torn up and burned. The bodies of the dead were thick, and badly burned men were heading for the quarterdeck, only to fall apparently dead or badly wounded."[1]

The *Arizona* sank in less than nine minutes, killing more than 1,100 sailors.

In addition to the war planes, the Japanese had sent several mini subs to the harbor. The U.S.S. *Oklahoma* was hit by several torpedoes and rolled over in the water, trapping more than 400 men inside. Both the U.S.S. *California* and U.S.S. *West Virginia* were sunk. The U.S.S. *Utah* capsized with more than 50 men on board. The U.S.S. *Maryland*, U.S.S. *Pennsylvania*, and U.S.S. *Tennessee* all suffered significant damage.

A second wave of warplanes struck after 8:30 A.M. and would last almost an hour. This time the attacks continued to pound the ships in the harbor, destroying the U.S.S. *Shaw* and the U.S.S. *Sotoyomo*. The U.S.S. *Nevada* tried to make it to sea but suffered too much damage and was beached to prevent it from sinking. In addition to targeting the ships, the Japanese fighters also attacked the nearby air fields.

Finally, shortly before 10:00 A.M., it was over. The Japanese flew away leaving Pearl Harbor a scene of horror and chaos. In all, 2,403 Americans were killed, 188 planes and eight battleships were either destroyed or badly damaged. The Japanese had lost twenty-nine aircraft and five midget subs. Despite the horrible loss of life and destruction, the attack had not completely taken out the Pacific Fleet. All the aircraft carriers had been out to sea, the submarines had survived virtually intact and Pearl Harbor itself was still usable. Even so, the attack crippled the U.S. Navy's capability for the immediate future. It also gave America no choice but to declare war on Japan.

The attack on Pearl Harbor was the result of long-brewing tensions. In 1931, Japan had invaded the Chinese province of Manchuria over the protests of the United States. Later in the decade, Japan joined the dictator Adolf Hitler's Nazi Germany and the dictator Benito Mussolini's Italy in what was called the Axis Alliance.

America tried to solve its differences with Japan diplomatically and through economic pressure, such as refusing to sell Japan's oil. But the Japanese leadership resisted and saw the embargoes as a direct threat. Rather than give in, Japan had made plans to go to war with America. But instead of officially declaring war, they started the conflict with the surprise attack on Pearl Harbor.

The American public was horrified and outraged. Up until the attack, most Americans had wanted to stay out of war. They didn't want to fight Japan in Asia or Germany in

Europe. But after Pearl Harbor, that changed. Never before had Americans been so united.

On December 8, 1941 President Franklin Delano Roosevelt addressed Congress. He asked for a declaration of war, calling the events at Pearl Harbor a "day that shall live in infamy." By the end of the day, the United States had declared war on Japan. Because of the Axis Alliance, Germany and Italy then declared war on the United States. World War II had begun.

The animosity towards Japan was unbridled. When Vice Admiral William F. Halsey viewed the destruction at Pearl Harbor, he fumed, "Before we're through with 'em, the Japanese language will be spoken only in hell!"[2]

But with the United States also involved in a war against Germany, America had to split its military resources. Even before the attack on Pearl Harbor, many political leaders had believed war was inevitable. Hitler was determined to control Europe and had amassed a strong army. There were rumors that Germany was working on a super weapon. Which is why, ironically, on December 6, 1941, the day before the Japanese attack, President Roosevelt had agreed to fund a secret project to build a nuclear bomb. At the time, experts disagreed whether such a weapon was even possible. But Roosevelt was willing to set aside a staggering $2 billion to find out.

Over the next four years, a group of top scientists would work in secret to build an atomic bomb. And when they finally succeeded, it would bring unimaginable destruction to Japan and a controversy that rages to this day.

To many people in the 1940s, the idea of a super weapon that could kill untold thousands of people was the stuff of science fiction. And as it happens, the atomic bomb was chillingly described in a 1944 short story called *Deadline*. Although it was written by Clive Cartmill, the idea for the story came from John W. Campbell, Jr., the editor of a popular science fiction magazine called *Astounding* (now called *Analog*.)

Campbell was not only an editor and a science fiction writer in his own right, he was also a science buff who loved to read technical journals. He was aware that a method had been developed to produce fissionable U-235. That prompted him in 1939 to write an editorial in his magazine commenting that with scientists having uncovered the secrets of fission and with war raging in Europe as Hitler tried to conquer the continent, he hoped that the world could get through the conflict without using a nuclear weapon.

What Campbell didn't know was that less than two years later, J. Robert Oppenheimer would be assembling an international team to create exactly such a weapon. Which is why after *Deadline* was published in March 1944, FBI agents showed up at Campbell's office demanding to know the source of the information contained in the short story and ordering the editor not to run any more stories about the development or potential destructiveness of nuclear weapons.

At first, Campbell couldn't figure out why the FBI was so concerned. He later discovered that some of the scientists at Los Alamos had subscriptions for his magazine. When they discussed *Deadline* and how accurate the story was, it prompted federal agents to pay Campbell a visit. It also resulted in Cartmill being put under surveillance.

Refusing to be intimidated, Campbell told the agents that it was no secret that the government was trying to develop an atomic weapon. He also pointed out that the public might become more suspicious if he suddenly stopped publishing stories about possible nuclear war. But a little over a year after *Deadline* was published the world would learn that the fictional horrors described by Cartmill were horrifyingly real.

In 1938 Italian physicist Enrico F
Nobel Prize for producing radioac

Fermi determined that during fission, neutrons were emitted from the atom's nucleus, effectively splitting it. That meant it would be possible to create a chain reaction that would result in an atomic explosion.

The "Italian Navigator"

At the turn of the twentieth century, scientist Marie Curie showed that radiation came from within the atom of a cell of uranium or other elements. This discovery was absolutely revolutionary and would be the basis for modern physics and the atomic age.

In the decades that followed Curie's discovery, many other scientists began studying atoms. In 1934 an Italian physicist named Enrico Fermi bombarded atoms with neutrons, particles that have no electrical charge and low energy. The experiments produced radioactive atoms. Fermi believed he had created new transuranic elements, or elements that have a higher atomic number than uranium. For this work, Fermi would win the Nobel Prize in physics in 1938. But what Fermi did not realize was that he had actually split the atom.

A year after Fermi received the Nobel Prize, two German scientists, Otto Hahn and Fritz Strassman, were doing similar experiments. They exposed uranium to neutrons. Based on Fermi's hypothesis, they expected the bombarded uranium nucleus to produce elements with an atomic number greater than uranium's 92. Instead, they found barium, which has an atomic number of 56.

Two other German physicists living in Denmark named Otto Frisch and Lise Meitner conducted their own experiments. They found the elements barium and krypton were produced when uranium absorbed neutrons. But in addition, Frisch and Meitner were able to explain the process. When the nucleus of an atom absorbs a neutron, the result is that the nucleus splits into two nuclei of "lighter" elements, or elements with lower atomic numbers. And when the nucleus splits, a great deal of energy is released. Frisch and Meitner called this process fission.

Shortly after this discovery, a Nobel Prize winning Danish physicist named Neils Bohr arrived in America to give a series of lectures at Princeton University. Bohr told his colleagues at the university about Frisch and Meitner's hypothesis. News of the theory spread among the scientific community. Before long, it reached Enrico Fermi, who was now working at Columbia University.

After taking his family to Sweden to accept his Nobel Prize, Fermi moved to New York instead of returning to Italy. Fermi's wife was Jewish. Now that Mussolini was in power, the government of Italy had enacted anti-Semitic laws, or laws that take away the rights of Jewish people. So to ensure her safety, they came to America.

Years later, Fermi would remember the moment he first heard about fission in January 1939. "Niels Bohr was on a lecture engagement in Princeton and I remember one after-

Further experiments confirmed that when the nucleus of an atom is bombarded with neutrons, it splits into two elements with lower atomic numbers, releasing a great deal of energy. They called this process fission.

Working with Otto Frisch, Lise Meitner (shown here) discovered that barium and krypton were produced when uranium absorbed neutrons.

noon Willis Lamb came back very excited and said that Bohr had leaked out great news. The great news that had leaked out was the discovery of fission and at least the outline of its interpretation."[1]

Later that month Fermi attended a conference on theoretical physics in Washington D.C. While there Fermi and Niels Bohr met and talked. Fermi suggested that during fission, neutrons might be emitted from the nucleus. This was a radical thought. If Fermi was right, that meant it was possible to create a fission chain reaction. That was because every time the nucleus of an atom split, it would enable the released neutrons to split other atoms. Such a chain reaction would release an almost unimaginable amount of energy, or nuclear power. If the chain reaction could be controlled, it could produce a new energy source. But if it happened too quickly, the result would be an atomic explosion.

Many scientists doubted this could be accomplished. But Hungarian physicist Leo Szilard had predicted the possibility of making an atomic bomb several years earlier. He was so sure that in July 1934, Szilard applied for an atomic bomb patent, meaning he wanted to "own" the rights. In the application, Szilard specifically described how neutrons would be used to start a chain reaction that would lead to an explosion. The application was approved. That meant Szilard was legally recognized as the inventor of the atomic bomb. Szilard's goal was not to make money. He gave the patent to the British War Office in 1936 because he did not want Germany to be the first to develop such a weapon.

Szilard, who was Jewish, moved to England in 1935 to get away from Nazi Germany's growing control over Eastern Europe. Three years later, he moved to America. After he learned about the discovery of fission, Szilard became convinced that it was only a matter of time before a bomb was made based on this discovery. He set out to convince the U.S. government to make fission a top priority.

But few people in America knew who Szilard was. So he turned to the most famous scientist in the world for help. Szilard asked Albert Einstein to write a letter with him to then President Franklin Roosevelt. The letter was sent in August. In it, Einstein warned Roosevelt that "it may become possible to set up a nuclear chain reaction in a large mass of uranium, by which vast amounts of power and large quantities of new radium-like elements would be generated. Now it appears almost certain that this could be achieved in the immediate future."[2]

Einstein's letter stressed Szilard's belief that Germany was already working on such a weapon. He wrote, "I understand that Germany has actually stopped the sale of uranium from the Czechoslovakian mines which she has taken over."[3]

Einstein wrote two more letters in 1940, again requesting research money. Other scientists also appealed to the President. Finally, on December 6, 1941 Roosevelt approved the funding. After the attack on Pearl Harbor the very next day, the research suddenly took on much greater importance.

Enrico Fermi was appointed as the leader of a research team that included Leo Szilard. Their assignment was to develop the first nuclear reactor. To accomplish that, they needed to achieve a *controllable* chain reaction. In other words, they needed to split an atom without creating an explosion.

They conducted their experiments at the University of Chicago. Fermi needed to develop a way to slow down the fission process in the "atomic pile." The atomic pile was the core of the reactor. In the core were layers of graphite, a type of carbon that is also used in lead pencils. Interspersed between the graphite was uranium which would be used to create fission. He discovered that rods made of the element cadmium would absorb neutrons. So the cadmium rods were inserted into the atomic pile to slow down the chain reaction and removed to speed it back up again.

On December 2, 1942, Fermi and Szilard were ready to test their theory. Everyone on the team was nervous. If Fermi was wrong, half of Chicago could be destroyed in a massive explosion. They removed some of the cadmium rods and the chain reaction began. When they removed more, the reaction became self-sustaining. The team could increase, and decrease, the amount of energy resulting from the chain reaction simply by adjusting the number of rods in the atomic pile. Finally, the uranium reached "critical mass," which is the level of fission necessary to trigger a self-sustaining chain reaction. Fermi had just built the first nuclear reactor.

It was a momentous achievement. The team sent a coded message to Washington D.C. "The Italian navigator has just landed in the new world."[4] The race to build the atomic bomb had officially started.

FOR YOUR INFORMATION

The Manhattan Project might have never happened had it not been for the revolutionary discoveries of physicists in the early twentieth century. Originally, scientists envisioned that the atom was structured like a solar system, with the nucleus being the sun that was orbited by electrons.

But in 1919, New Zealand native Ernest Rutherford was working in his laboratory at England's Cambridge University when he detected another kind of particle being emitted by the nucleus. Unlike the electron, which has a slight negative charge, this particle had a positive charge so he called it a proton. But the proton created a new puzzle for scientists to solve.

Ernest Rutherford

The atomic number, which is the number of protons in an atom, was less than the known atomic mass of the atom. For example, helium has an atomic number of two, meaning it has two protons, but an atomic mass of four. Since electrons virtually have no weight because they are a pure electrical charge, it meant that there was another kind of particle in the atom that was giving it the known atomic mass.

Some scientists thought that perhaps there were "hidden" protons and electrons in the nucleus. But Rutherford had a more controversial suggestion – that there was actually a third, as of yet undiscovered particle in the atom that had mass but no charge. But at the time, he had no way to prove such a theory.

After World War I ended, a young researcher named James Chadwick came to work with Rutherford in his Cambridge laboratory, researching radioactivity. He specifically set out to discover whether or not Rutherford was right about a third particle, and eventually developed an experiment that proved the theory correct. He named the uncharged particles neutrons and determined they weighed slightly more than protons.

This new picture of atoms had an immediate, dramatic impact. Physicists quickly discovered that neutrons were perfectly sited to bombard other nuclei. Because it had no charge, a neutron would not be repelled by either protons or electrons. Scientists would eventually use neutrons to bombard uranium to split its nucleus, opening the door for the development of atomic weapons.

J. Robert Oppenheimer was appointed to run the top secret Manhattan Project.

One of Oppenheimer's most important duties was to recruit scientists to work on the project. In the end he would oversee nearly two hundred scientists working at the Los Alamos Laboratory in New Mexico. It was Oppenheimer who came up with the cover story that the scientists were working on a new rocket.

Racing Against the Clock

In August 1942, the Manhattan Engineer District was formed to oversee the effort to build an atomic weapon. That's why it became known as the Manhattan Project. In September of that same year, General Leslie R. Groves was put in charge of the project. Known for being exacting and organized, Groves wasted no time moving forward. Groves and others believed Germany was also working on developing an atomic weapon. It seemed clear that whoever succeeded first would win the war.

Ironically, Germany never really had the resources to seriously pursue an atomic weapon. After the war it was discovered that top Nazi officials were never fully briefed on the potential of such a bomb. But in the eyes of the American military, we were in a race against the clock.

One of Grove's first decisions was to appoint physicist J. Robert Oppenheimer as Scientific Director of the Manhattan Project. Groves considered Oppenheimer a genius, and together they picked out the location for a new laboratory the project needed. Oppenheimer suggested a remote desert area in New Mexico. He remembered the area from having attended a summer camp at a school there as a young boy and thought it was remote enough to ensure their secrecy. Groves agreed, and they negotiated to buy the school. The owners were happy to sell the buildings and property for $440,000 because they had found it difficult finding teachers because of the war. Los Alamos, New Mexico, would become the site of the main laboratory where the bomb would be designed and constructed.

Two other locations were also selected for secret laboratories working on other aspects of the project. At Oak Ridge, Tennessee, a nuclear reactor was built, along with a plant for producing and purifying large quantities of uranium. Originally, a site near Knoxville had been considered. But Groves decided against building any production facilities near major populations. According to Richard Rhodes, author of *The Making of the Atomic Bomb*, Groves worried that a nuclear accident would "cause the loss of life and damage health in the area" and, perhaps even more importantly for the military man, would "wipe out all semblance of security in the project."[1] Three reactors were also built in Hanford, Washington. These would eventually be used to produce plutonium.

Each secret site became a self-contained small city, with houses for the workers, a bus system, grocery stores and everything else those working on the project needed. It was important to isolate those involved in the project as much as possible so that word of the project didn't leak out. That meant that many families living near the designated sites were forced to move. To build the Washington complex, the small towns of Richland, White Bluffs and Hanford literally disappeared. It was a sacrifice that those in charge of the Manhattan Project believed was necessary to maintain security.

Oppenheimer's next task was to recruit scientists. He traveled the country hoping to talk the best physicists and engineers into moving to New Mexico to work on the design of the bomb. Almost two hundred scientists agreed to join the project. By 1943, all three sites were up and running. Ever mindful of security, Oppenheimer wrote Groves a letter, suggesting a cover story for the obvious activity happening in Los Alamos.

"We propose that it be let known that the Los Alamos Project is working on a new type of rocket and that...this is a largely electrical device...We further believe that the remoteness of the site for such a development and the secrecy which has surrounded the project would both be appropriate, and that the circumstance that a good deal of work is in fact being done on rockets, together with the appeal of the word, makes this story one which is both exciting and credible."[2]

Now that the facilities were ready, scientists tackled the first obstacle: manufacturing enough of the uranium 235 isotope to make a weapon. An isotope is a form of an element that has a different number of neutrons. While an isotope has the same chemical properties as the element, because of the different number of neutrons its radioactivity may be different. Uranium 235 is obtained from uranium ore, a naturally occurring rock. Uranium 238 is another isotope that is in ore, but in much larger quantities. On average, U-235 makes up only 1% of uranium ore, while U-238 makes up the other 99%. But U-238 is not capable of fission because it cannot sustain a chain reaction. That presented two problems for Oppenheimer and the others. The first was separating the two isotopes from one another. The second was to obtain enough U-235 for their experiments. To do that, a huge amount of uranium ore needed to be processed.

The first method used to separate the isotopes was a cyclotron. Invented by Ernest Lawrence at the University of California at Berkeley Laboratories in the 1930s, the cyclotron separates particles by spinning them in a machine at very high speeds. The uranium was put in a mixture that was electrically charged. Inside the cyclotron was a magnet. When spun, the lighter U-235 would pass closer to the magnet and be collected. The heavier U-238 atoms would spin further away and not be trapped by the magnet. But this process had many problems. Most notably, the magnet would also attract dirt and would have to be constantly cleaned. This caused frequent delays, time Grove felt the project didn't have. Plus, after spending millions of dollars, the Berkeley team was only able to produce about a gram of U-235

So a second method was developed. Groves ordered a "separation facility" to be built at the Oak Ridge, Tennessee location. The facility would use "gaseous diffusion" to separate the two isotopes. The technique was actually simple in theory. A membrane would act as a diffusion barrier. Because they are lighter, the U-235 molecules passed through more quickly, leaving the heavier, and more slowly moving, U-238 behind. By repeating the process several times, scientists were able to separate the two isotopes.

While uranium was still the primary focus as a fuel source for an atomic weapon, another element was also being studied. Physicists working at the University of California at Berkeley were busy studying the properties of plutonium, a transuranium element which had only been discovered in 1941 by Glenn Seaborg. Like uranium, plutonium had an unstable isotope, P-239, that was capable of producing a fission chain-

Among the scientists Lawrence worked with around the clock at Los Alamos Laboratory were Erico Fermi (center) and Isidor Rabi (right). Once they developed potential atomic fuel in U-235 and plutonium-239, it would still take two years to develop the first atomic weapon.

Ernest Lawrence (left) invented the cyclotron, a machine that separates isotopes of an element.

reaction. More remarkably, Seaborg discovered that U-238 could be transformed into P-239. All he had to do was put it in a nuclear reactor. Once in the reactor, the uranium isotope would "pick up" extra neutrons.

Now that the project had two potential fuels for its weapon, the next challenge was to design and build a bomb. Then it would have to be tested. This aspect of the project was done at the Los Alamos Laboratory, which opened in April 1943. For the next two years, scientists and engineers would literally work around the clock. It was Oppenheimer's job to coordinate the work at the three sites, manage the more than three thousand people working on the project, and oversee the actual development of the bomb at Los Alamos. But in less than two years, the team would be ready to detonate the world's first atomic weapon and forever change the course of human history.

The Mars Rover

Although the laboratory at Los Alamos began as part of a top-secret government project, it has since become one of the world's most respected research centers. Controlled by the U.S. Department of Energy but run by the University of California, the Los Alamos National Laboratory is responsible for maintaining the nation's nuclear stockpile but also conducts a variety of scientific research including environmental, health and energy issues. Ironically, the technology developed through the lab's work to improve the materials used in nuclear weaponry has resulted in a number of important products that have improved humanity's quality of life, including smaller, longer-lasting batteries, efficient fuel cells, stronger composite materials and all-carbon prosthetics and joint replacements. The National Laboratory also participated in the Human Genome Project, in which scientists from all over the world worked together to "map" the DNA sequence of human beings.

Not surprisingly, the scientists and students working at the National Laboratory are also very concerned with the health and environmental dangers posed by both long-term and short-term radiation. They are also working on ways to protect civilians from possible terrorist attacks using nuclear, biological or chemical weapons.

Perhaps more surprising is the National Laboratory's contribution to the space program. Scientists there have already analyzed data sent from satellite. And when NASA's planned Mars Science Laboratory rover launches in 2009, two of the eight instruments on board will be under the control of scientists at Los Alamos. The rover's mission will be to explore for evidence of past or present life. The laboratory's laser unit will reveal the chemical composition of the rocks and soil it zaps. The advantage of using a laser is that the rover can analyze objects from far away and not have to travel close by. The other instrument, an X-ray diffraction machine, will provide analysis of minerals.

Winston Churchill was the British Minister during World War II. A orator, Churchill's speeches were keeping up the morale of Londoner through daily bombings by German

The plutonium bomb was nicknamed Fat Man *in honor of Churchill. After the war, Churchill published a six-volume book called* The Second World War *for which he won a Nobel Prize for Literature.*

"Little Boy" and "Fat Man"

Because the Manhattan Project was developing two potential fuels, the first using uranium and the other using plutonium, two different bomb designs were developed. That was because of subtle differences in the chemical properties of the two elements. In the uranium bomb, which was nicknamed *Little Boy*, the fissionable material needed to be squeezed together. So a wad of U-235 was projected down a modified gun barrel into another glob of the isotope. When they combined, it created a critical mass that initiated a fission chain reaction that set off an atomic explosion.

The other bomb was called *Fat Man,* named after British Prime Minister Winston Churchill. It used plutonium as fuel. The plutonium was surrounded by a ring of explosives. When the explosives detonated, the plutonium imploded, or was compressed inward, which would result in a nuclear blast.

In July 1943, 250 scientists were living in Los Alamos, which was also known as *The Hill*. By July 1945, there were more than 2,500 scientists, housed in dormitories like college students. One former resident said it looked like a Gold Rush mining camp. FBI agents were also assigned to the town to make sure nobody got in or left unless authorized.

Despite the seriousness of the project, there was also a great deal of enthusiasm in Los Alamos. Melvin Brooks, a University of Chicago chemical engineer recalled to *Newsday*, "It was exciting. It was probably the last of a pioneering kind of spirit."[1]

Austrian physicist Victor Weisskopf agreed. "It was so amazing because everybody who was anybody was there. We all sort of lived in an excited state."[2]

At least twelve current or future Nobel Prize winners were on the team, which further inspired the younger scientists on the team.

Interestingly, during the years the Los Alamos team worked to design the bombs, there was little if any discussion about the moral implications of whether or not such a potentially deadly weapon should be made. Brooks explained the scientists' mindset to *Newsday*: "We knew what the objective was. We knew what it was, and why it was being built and what it was going to be used for. There was never a question."[3]

Arthur Wahl, a chemist who co-discovered plutonium observed to reporter Earl Lane, "We did not sit around discussing the ethics of the bomb; we wanted to make it. I think it was the right thing. Knowing what I know now, I'd do the same thing."[4]

Many of the scientists at Los Alamos were Europeans who had fled their countries to escape Hitler. Now in America, they were anxious to do whatever they could to help the Allies win the war.

According to the scientists who worked on the project, everywhere they turned it seemed Oppenheimer was there. He made it a point to visit every lab and take an interest in what work was being done. Perhaps his greatest gift was that he was able to settle disputes among the strong-willed scientists and keep the project on track. Ben Diven, who worked at Los Alamos, said in a *Newsday* interview, "I don't know if it would have worked with someone other than Oppenheimer."[5]

Not only were the scientists working, on average, 14-hour-work days, they were also under incredible pressure. As previously noted, the Germans had never made developing an atomic weapon a priority. But as far as the scientists knew, they were in a life and death race. "There was a clear and present danger that the Nazis would get the bomb first," Weisskopf recalled to Earl Lane.[6]

By early 1945, there was enough uranium and plutonium fuel so that the scientists at Los Alamos could test a device. Hanford sent a ball of plutonium to New Mexico. It was approximately the size of an orange. On July 13, a plutonium bomb was assembled and brought to a test site in the New Mexico desert on the Alamagordo Bombing Range. The code name for the test was Trinity. But bad weather forced Oppenheimer to delay the test for three days.

Finally, in the predawn hours of July 16, 1945, the scientists were ready to set off the bomb. At exactly 5:29:45 A.M. the bomb was detonated. The flash of light from the explosion was visible over 250 miles away and released more than four times the heat of the interior of the sun. The tower holding the bomb was vaporized and melted the nearby desert sand into green glass now called Trinitite. A mile away, exposed surfaces heated to 750 degrees. Ten miles away, witnesses would later recount it felt as if they were standing in front of a roaring fire.

Within seconds the resulting fireball was almost half a mile wide, expanding seven miles into the night sky in a mushroom shape. The cloud had a haunting blue glow from the radiation being given off. Forty seconds after detonation, a gust of wind from the bomb reached the observation bunker located six miles away. The sound was deafening and broke windows 120 miles away.

In all, the explosive power of the bomb was measured to be equivalent to nearly 19,000 tons of TNT. The blast was four times as strong as the scientists anticipated. And it was at that moment that the enormous deadly potential of the weapon began to sink in. Oppenheimer is reported to have quoted from the *Bhagavad Gita*, an epic Hindu poem. "If the radiance of a thousand suns were to burst at once into the sky that would be like the splendor of the Mighty One... I am become death, the shatterer of worlds."[7]

Joe McKibben was the physicist who actually set the bomb off. He was two miles away from the explosion. He recalled to the *Seattle Times* that once he saw the purple red fireball rushing into the sky, "I knew the war would soon be over."[8]

4

Just four hours after the successful detonation of *Fat Man*, *Little Boy* was boarded onto the U.S.S. *Indianapolis* in San Francisco. The cruiser's top secret mission was to take the bomb to the South Pacific Island of Tinian. On the way back from delivering the bomb, the *Indianapolis* was torpedoed by a Japanese submarine. Because its mission had been so top secret, nobody noticed when the cruiser didn't return to port. The surviving crew men floated in the ocean for days. Over 500 were eaten by sharks before a plane finally spotted them and called for a rescue.

Now that the bomb had been created, a disagreement arose on whether or not it should ever be used. Franklin Roosevelt had died in April 1945 and Harry S. Truman assumed the Presidency. A month later, Hitler committed suicide and Germany unconditionally surrendered, ending the war in Europe. But the Japanese promised to fight to the death.

Military experts at the time estimated that it would cost over several hundred thousand American lives to successfully invade Japan, which still had 2 million troops and 8,000 kamikaze aircraft. The Japanese fatalities would probably be even higher. The Allies had been bombing Tokyo, causing terrible destruction without it diminishing the Japanese resolve.

A *Seattle Times* article quoted Air Force General Hap Arnold as saying, "We had had 100,000 people killed in Tokyo in one night of (conventional) bombs and it had seemingly no effect whatsoever. It destroyed the Japanese cities, yes, but their morale was not affected as far as we could tell, not at all.

So it seemed quite necessary, if we could, to shock them into action" with the atomic bomb.[9]

Now that the bomb was a reality, several scientists, including Enrico Fermi, urged the U.S. government to try to persuade Japan to surrender by giving them a demonstration of the bomb's power. Some suggested an atomic bomb be detonated over Tokyo Bay to give the Emperor a chance to surrender and save lives. But because there were only two available bombs, that idea was rejected.

Instead, on July 26, 1945, the United States, Great Britain, and China issued the Potsdam Declaration. It demanded that Japan unconditionally surrender immediately or be subjected to "prompt and utter destruction." The Japanese Prime Minister responded by saying his country chose to ignore the Declaration.

Although Truman had the power to stop the military from using the atomic weapon, he chose not to. The plan to drop the bomb was set in motion. On August 5, 1945 President Truman gave his final approval to use *Little Boy*. The people of Japan could not imagine the horror that was about to befall them.

Because of its remoteness and low population, the desert proved to be a perfect place to conduct the top-secret work necessary to develop the atomic bomb. After World War II ended, a huge expanse of desert called the Nevada Test Site would be set aside so that the U.S. government could conduct a series of nuclear weapons tests during the Cold War arms race with Russia. About the size of Rhode Island, the 1,375 square mile test site is only a little over an hour's drive from Las Vegas and is part of the Western Shoshone Indian Territory.

A Bomb at the Nevada Test Site

President Harry Truman officially founded the Nevada Test Site on January 11, 1951. The first atomic test, called Operation Ranger, occurred there just two weeks later. Between then and when the site was shut down in 1992, over 900 atomic explosions were detonated. Initially, in the 1950s, these tests were conducted above ground. But later, as concerns over the health hazards of releasing too much radioactivity into the open air increased, the tests were conducted underground. The power of the explosions left the ground above the tests ruptured, making the area resemble the pockmarked landscape of the moon.

Since nuclear testing was disbanded in 1992, the Nevada Test Site is now controlled by the Department of Energy (DOE) that uses the area for a variety of programs, including emergency response training, conventional weapons testing, and waste management and environmental technology studies.

Adjacent to the Nevada Testing Ground is a top-secret military base that is known as Area 51. In 1947, residents in the town of Roswell, New Mexico, regularly reported seeing strange lights in the sky and one night claimed a UFO had crashed nearby. The official explanation that a metallic weather balloon had crashed was dismissed by many as a U.S. government cover-up of the fact that aliens had landed on earth. There was also speculation that the American military was using advanced technology from alien spacecraft in developing its own planes.

From the 1950s through the 1990s, the Air Force Flight Test Center tested many classified weapons and aircraft in Area 51, including the U-2 spyplane. But as concern over the high levels of radiation in the area persisted and the fact the base was no longer a secret, the Air Force abandoned its base at Area 51 and has moved to a new undisclosed base in Utah known only as Area 6413 where the next generation of military aircraft is being developed and tested.

Believing it would ultimately save both American and Japanese lives in the long-run, President Harry Truman approved dropping the atomic bomb on Hiroshima.

On August 5, 1945, Little Boy *was dropped on Hiroshima. Four days later a second bomb was dropped on Nagasaki. Over 175,000 people died and on August 14 Japan surrendered unconditionally, ending World War II.*

Fallout

Once the decision was made to use the bomb, the next question was where to drop it. A Target Committee was formed under the control of General Groves. They developed several guidelines. First, they wanted a city that had not already been hurt by Allied bombing. Next, they wanted a city with a geographical layout that would allow for maximized destruction from the bomb's blast wave. Four cities were on the final list. Kyoto was first followed by Hiroshima, Kokura and Higata. But Secretary of War Henry Stimson vetoed taking any action against Kyoto. The city was an ancient capital of Japan and had great historical and cultural significance to the Japanese. Stimson felt bombing that city would permanently embitter the Japanese against America. So Nagasaki was added to the list and Kyoto removed.

In the end, the military chose Hiroshima, where 43,000 Japanese soldiers were stationed, as the first target. The second target, should Japan still refuse to surrender, would be Nagasaki. Nagasaki was an industrial city. Its shipyards had built many of Japan's warships and its factories had made the torpedoes used at Pearl Harbor.

Almost a year before the successful Trinity test, General Groves was already laying the groundwork for dropping the bomb. In September 1944, he assigned Lieutenant Colonel Paul Tibbets, Jr. the task of organizing and training a squad whose mission it would be to drop an atomic bomb. The bomb would be carried in a B-29 and Tibbets had flown more hours in a B-29 than anyone in the military. The plane that would drop the bomb needed to be specially outfitted. *Little Boy* weighed 5 tons so a special frame needed to be constructed from which to suspend the bomb.

On August 5, Colonel Tibbets had the name *Enola Gay* painted on the plane holding the bomb. At 2:30 A.M. on August 6, Tibbets and his crew took off for *Special Bombing Mission #13*. In addition to Tibbets were co-pilot Captain Bob Lewis, and three others. The target where they would drop *Little Boy* was the Aioi Bridge, located in the center of Hiroshima.

At 9:15:15 A.M., the bomb was released. Forty-three seconds later it exploded 1900 feet above the city. Later, Captain Lewis would recall, "I don't believe anyone ever expected to look at a sight quite like that. Where we had seen a clear city two minutes earlier, we could now no longer see the city."[1] Almost two-thirds of the city was destroyed. Sixty thousand buildings were demolished by the force of the blast. It is estimated over 100,000 people were killed by the initial explosion. Tens of thousands more would die within five years from radiation poisoning.

A survivor would later recount in *Death in Life: Survivors of Hiroshima* that the people he saw "all had skin blackened by burns. They had no hair because their hair was burned, and at a glance you couldn't tell whether you were looking at them from in front or in back....Their skin—not only on their hands, but on their faces and bodies too—hung down.... Wherever I walked I met these people. Many of them died along the road—I can still picture them in my mind—like walking ghosts."[2]

On August 9, a copy of *Fat Man*, again with plutonium as its fuel, was dropped on Nagasaki. Although this bomb was more powerful than the one dropped on Hiroshima, Nagasaki's terrain helped limit the damage. Even so, another 75,000 people would die from the explosion.

The devastation was unimaginable. Faced with the prospect of more attacks, Japan unconditionally surrendered on August 14, 1945. The war was over, but the controversy was just beginning. In the years since Hiroshima, arguments have raged whether America should have given Japan more opportunities to surrender. Many feel that had the Japanese leaders been shown the power of the bomb, they might have surrendered without the staggering loss of civilian life. But those who gave the orders to use the weapon firmly believed that ultimately hundreds of thousands, if not millions of lives of both Americans and Japanese were actually saved by using the atomic weapons.

Edward Teller, who worked on the Manhattan Project, and was later the developer of the even more deadly hydrogen bomb, believes that it was absolutely necessary to develop the bomb. But, he told the *Seattle Times*, "I have one very great regret in connection with the bomb. We should have worked out, in detail, a way to demonstrate it. To work out an alternative was the scientists' job. I generally like the idea of a nuclear-bomb explosion over Tokyo Bay, at 8 P.M. in the evening, with a clear sky. It would light up the whole sky for 10 million people to see. They would hear a sound like they had never heard before. And we would say, "'Give up, or we will use this on your cities.' The emperor would have seen it."[3]

Physicist Phillip Morrison agrees but stressed to *Newsday* that there's no easy answer. "I think we should have pushed harder for a warning. But I trusted my leadership. I think we were wrong in going ahead, but arguably wrong."[4]

Oppenheimer's feelings are summed up by a comment he made to Truman a year after the war ended. "Mr. President, I have blood on my hands." However, Truman did not share his guilt. According to an interview with Dean Acheson in *Newsweek*, Truman felt confident the right decision had been made. Acheson says the President told him, "He [Oppenheimer] didn't set that bomb off. I did. This kind of sniveling makes me sick."[5]

Regardless of whatever one's political or moral views on the bombing of Hiroshima and Nagasaki, what cannot be disputed is the unprecedented scientific, technological and engineering feat achieved by those who worked on the Manhattan Project. It is especially impressive when remembering only six years had elapsed from the discovery of fission to the Trinity test.

Most of the scientists who helped develop the bomb went on to enjoy distinguished careers. Many stayed at Los Alamos, which has become an important national research center. Others, like Enrico Fermi, returned to their teaching and research jobs at Universities, often to work on peacetime uses for nuclear energy. Many became activists who worked to stop the proliferation, or increase, of nuclear weapons. But all the men and women who had worked on the Manhattan Project knew one thing for certain. They had harnessed the power of the atom and in so doing forever changed the course of human history, for better or worse. With this discovery came a great responsibility.

As J. Robert Oppenheimer noted, "The atomic bomb made the prospect of future war unendurable. It has led us up those last few steps to the mountain pass; and beyond there is a different country."[6]

While nuclear weapons continue to pose a threat to the world's safety and security, scientists the world over are researching ways to make atomic power work for mankind's benefit. In 1953, President Dwight D. Eisenhower proposed establishing an international agency that would promote peacetime uses of Nuclear energy. As a result, the International Atomic Energy Agency was formed four years later.

Three Mile Island

As technology advances, more and more peaceful uses for atomic energy and by-products are being found. The best known are using nuclear reactors to generate electricity as the world's supply of natural gas, coal and oil becomes ever more depleted. But as the accidents at Three Mile Island and Chernobyl make clear, human error could turn these positive uses into tragedies if extreme care is not taken.

Radioisotopes, which are radioactive forms of elements, have become important tools in medicine for fighting cancer. The reason radiation treatments have become so widely used is that doctors can control where exactly the radiation is directed. So when isotopes are zapped into a person's body, it can be aimed directly at the tumor. So even though the cancer cells are being destroyed by the radiation, the surrounding healthy tissue is left mostly untouched. Radioisotopes are also used in manufacturing to make luminous paints that "glow" in the dark.

Scientists are also seeking ways to use radioactive materials to preserve food. It has already been shown that exposing potatoes to radiation will extend the time they stay fresh. However, researchers are still trying to prevent the loss of nutritional value or the change of taste that can accompany such a process. But if radiation can be used to prevent food products such as wheat flour, fruits, meats and vegetables from going bad, it could have an enormous impact in reducing world hunger and improving the quality of life for millions, especially in developing nations.

Chronology

1932	James Chadwick proves the existence of neutrons
1934	Enrico Fermi succeeds in splitting an atom; Szilard applies for a patent for an atomic bomb
1939	Otto Frisch and Lise Meitner develop theory of fission; Leo Szilard enlists Albert Einstein to write President Roosevelt and urge him to pursue the development of an atomic powered weapon; Germany invades Poland, starting World War II
1940	The University of California at Berkeley begins construction of a giant cyclotron under the direction of Ernest Lawrence
1941	President Roosevelt approves development of an atomic bomb; Glenn Seaborg discovers plutonium
1942	Enrico Fermi creates a controlled nuclear reaction; the Manhattan Project is officially formed; J. Robert Oppenheimer is named director of the Manhattan Project
1943	The Los Alamos Laboratory opens. Research and production facilities for the Manhattan Project are also built in Oak Ridge, Tennessee and Hanford, Washington
1944	A second nuclear reactor is built in Tennessee; Lieutenant Colonel Paul Tibbets is chosen to train a unit to "deliver" the bomb
1945	On July 16, the U.S. explodes the first atomic bomb in New Mexico; On August 6 an atomic bomb is dropped on Hiroshima; a uranium bomb is dropped on Nagasaki three days later. Japan surrenders
1946	The United Nations General Assembly establishes the Atomic Energy Commission
1954	Scientists succeed in creating a hydrogen bomb that is thousands of times more powerful than the bomb dropped on Hiroshima

Timeline in History

1896	French physicist Antoine Becquerel discovers radioactivity
1909	Sir Ernest Rutherford constructs the first nuclear model of the atom, setting the foundation for modern physics
1931	Harold C. Urey discovers deuterium, the name for heavy hydrogen
1933	Adolf Hitler becomes chancellor of Germany, prompting many scientists to emigrate to Britain and the United states
1938	Otto Hahn and Fritz Strassmann discover fission
1939	Germany invades Poland, starting World War II
1945	World War II ends
1949	Soviet Union explodes its first atomic bomb in Kazakhstan on August 29
1962	The Cuban Missile Crisis brings world to the brink of nuclear war
1964	China develops nuclear weapons, becoming the fifth country with atomic warheads
1968	The United Nations drafts the Treaty on the Non-Proliferation of Nuclear Weapons, which is signed by the five countries possessing nuclear weapons: the U.S., Britain, Russia, France and China and other non-nuclear countries
1972	The U.S. and Soviet Union sign the first Strategic Arms Limitation Talks Treaty (also known as SALT I), which placed limits on the number of nuclear weapons each side could possess
1999	Rival countries India and Pakistan conduct nuclear weapons tests
2004	Iran may be able to make an atomic bomb
2005	North Korea claims to have the bomb

Chapter Notes

Chapter One
A Day of Infamy

1. EyeWitness to History, "Attack At Pearl Harbor, 1941," http://www.eye witnesstohistory.com/pearl.htm

2. Naval Historical Center, "Pearl Harbor Raid, 7 December 1941: Japanese Forces in the Pearl Harbor Attack," http://www.history.navy.mil/ photos/events/wwii-pac/pearlhbr/ph-ja1.htm

Chapter 2
The "Italian Navigator"

1. Biography.ms, "Enrico Fermi," http://enrico-fermi.biography.ms/

2. EWorld, "Albert Einstein's Letters to President Franklin Delano Roosevelt," http://hypertextbook.com/ eworld/einstein.shtml#first

3. Ibid.

4. PBS, *A Science Odessey*, "Fermi creates controlled nuclear reaction," http://www.pbs.org/wgbh/aso/databank/ entries/dp42fe.html

Chapter Three
Racing Against the Clock

1. Richard Rhodes, *The Making of the Atomic Bomb* (New York: Simon & Schuster, Inc., 1986).

2. Nuclearfiles.org, "J. Robert Oppenheimer's memo for General Leslie R. Groves, April 30, 1943," http://nuclearfiles.org/redocuments/ 1943/430430-opp-groves.html

Chapter Four
"Little Boy" and "Fat Man"

1. Earl Lane, *Newsday*, "Hiroshima. The Manhattan Project Scientists," July 17, 1995.

2. Fred Bruning, *Newsday*, "50 Years Later, Still Struggling With Its Impact: The Birth of the Bomb," July 16, 1995.

3. Earl Lane, *Newsday*, "Hiroshima. The Manhattan Project Scientists," July 17, 1995.

4. Ibid.

5. Earl Lane, *Newsday*, "Tinkering In The Beast's Lair," Jul 18, 1995, p. B19.

6. Ibid.

7. The Quotes and Sayings Database, "Life is Beautiful," http:// www.quotesandsayings.com/qgita.htm

8. *Seattle Times*, "50 Years from Trinity. Part I: Trinity Site New Mexico," http:// seattletimes.nwsource.com/trinity/ articles/part1.html

9. *Seattle Times*, "50 Years from Trinity. Bomb History Still Bears Bitterness," http:// seattletimes.nwsource. com/trinity/articles/closer1.html

Chapter Five
Fallout

1. Ronald Takaki, *Hiroshima: Why America Dropped the Atomic Bomb* (New York: Little, Brown and Company, 1995), p. 43.

2. Robert Jay Lifton, *Death in Life: Survivors of Hiroshima* (New York: Random House, 1967) p. 27.

3. *Seattle Times*, "50 Years from Trinity. Bomb History Still Bears Bitterness," http:// seattletimes.nwsource. com/trinity/articles/closer1.htm

4. Earl Lane, *Newsday*, "Hiroshima: The Manhattan Project Scientists," July 17, 1995.

5. *Newsweek*, October 20, 1969, p. 71.

6. Richard Rhodes, *The Making of the Atomic Bomb* (New York: Simon & Schuster, Inc., 1986), p. 87.

For Further Reading

For Young Adults

Bankston, John. *Edward Teller and the Development of the Hydrogen Bomb.* Newark, Delaware: Mitchell Lane Publishers, 2004

Bankston, John. *Lise Meitner and the Atomic Bomb.* Newark, Delaware: Mitchell Lane Publishers, 2002.

Groueff, Stephane. *Manhattan Project: The Untold Story of the Making of the Atomic Bomb.* New York: Little Brown, 1967

Hughes, Jeff. *The Manhattan Project: Big Science and the Atom Bomb (Revolutions in Science).* New York: Columbia University Press, 2003.

Rhodes, Richard. *The Making of the Atomic Bomb.* New York: Simon & Schuster,1995.

Works Consulted

Badash, L. *Scientists and the Development of Nuclear Weapons: From Fission to the Limited Test Ban Treaty 1939-1963.* Atlantic Highlands, New Jersey: Humanities Press, 1995.

Bainbridge, K. *Trinity: Los Alamos publication (LA-6300-H).* Los Alamos Scientific Laboratory, 1976.

Bethe, H. A. *The Road from Los Alamos.* New York: Woodbury, New York: AIP Press, 1991.

Feis, H. *The Atomic Bomb and the End of World War II.* Princeton, New Jersey: Princeton University Press, 1966.

Groves, L. R. *Now It Can Be Told: The Story of the Manhattan Project.* Cambridge, Massachusetts: Da Capo Press, 1983.

Lane, Earl. *Newsday.* "Hiroshima: The Manhattan Project Scientists." July 17, 1995.

Lifton, Robert Jay. *Death in Life: Survivors of Hiroshima.* New York: Random House, 1967.

Nuclearfiles.org: "J. Robert Oppenheimer's memo for General Leslie R. Groves, April 30, 1943" http://nuclearfiles.org/redocuments/1943/430430-opp-groves.html

Rhodes, R. *The Making of the Atomic Bomb.* New York: Simon and Schuster, 1988.

Seaborg, Glenn T. *Adventures in the Atomic Age.* Berkeley, California: Farrar, Straus, & Giroux, 2001.

Seattle Times. "50 Years from Trinity. Bomb History Still Bears Bitterness." http://seattletimes.nwsource.com/trinity/articles/closer1.html

Seattle Times, "50 Years from Trinity. Part I: Trinity Site New Mexico." http://seattletimes.nwsource.com/trinity/articles/part1.html

Takaki, Ronald. *Hiroshima: Why America Dropped the Atomic Bomb.* New York: Little, Brown and Company, 1995.

On the Internet

KidsNet www.kids.net.au/encyclopedia/?p=ma/Manhattan_Project

Fact Monster: The Manhattan Project http://www.factmonster.com/ce6/sci/A0831533.html

National Atomic Musuem: The Manhattan Project http://www.atomicmuseum.com/tour/manhattanproject.cfm

Manhattan Project Heritage Preservation Association, Inc. http://www.childrenofthemanhattanproject.org/

Glossary

Cryptographer
(crip-TAH-gra-FUR)
someone who creates or breaks codes

Cyclotron
(SIGH-clo-tron)
a machine that accelerates charged particles

Element
(EL-uh-ment)
the simplest part into which something can be divided

Fission
(fi-ZHUN)
the splitting in two of the nucleus of an atom, resulting in a release of energy. The nucleus is split by striking it with a neutron

Fission chain reaction
(fi-ZHUN CHAYNE ree-ACK-shun)
What happens when neutrons released during fission hit the nuclei of other atoms, causing them to split, which releases more neutrons, causing more nuclei to split until a large amount of energy is released

Fusion
(FEW-zhun)
another type of nuclear reaction. In fusion, nuclei are combined to form a large nucleus, resulting in a release of energy

Hypothesis
(high-PAH- theh-SIS)
A theory or an idea

Implode
(im-PLODE)
when something collapses inward. The opposite of explosion, where something blows apart

Isotope
(EYE-so-tope)
one of two or more types of a chemical element that have the same atomic number but a different number of neutrons

Neutron
(NEW-tron)
a particle that makes up the nucleus that has no electrical charge

Nucleus
(NEW-clee-us), plural nuclei
the center of an atom that contains most of its mass. In all elements except hydrogen, the nucleus is made up of protons and neutrons

Patent
(PAT-ent)
Ownership of an invention

Radiation
(ray-dee-AY-shun)
a form of energy that can be categorized according to wavelength; the spectrum includes X-rays, radio waves, and infrared, ultraviolet, and visible light

Radioactivity
(RAY-dee-oh-ack-TI-vi-tee)
the spontaneous emission of radiation from the nucleus of an unstable isotope

Rationing
(ra-SHUN-ing)
limiting the amount of products you can buy

Transuranic
(TRANS-ur-an-ik)
A radioactive element made by artificial means that has a higher atomic number than uranium

Index